E 612
c.1
Cobb, Vicki.

Perk up your ears :
discover your sense of
c2001.

W9-BCF-232

**NRC** CASS COUNTY PUBLIC LIBRARY
400 E. MECHANIC
HARRISONVILLE, MO 64701

# Perk up your ears

## Discover Your Sense of Hearing

# hearing

VICKI COBB

*Illustrations by*

*Cynthia C. Lewis*

**NRC** CASS COUNTY PUBLIC LIBRARY
400 E. MECHANIC
HARRISONVILLE, MO 64701

The Millbrook Press
Brookfield, Connecticut

0 0022 0268083 7

The author takes full responsibility for the accuracy of the text, and gratefully acknowledges the technical assistance of Professor Lawrence D. Rosenblum of the University of California, Riverside, and his graduate assistant Michael S. Gordon.

Published by The Millbrook Press, Inc.
2 Old New Milford Road
Brookfield, CT   06804
www.millbrookpress.com

Library of Congress Cataloging-in-Publication Data
Cobb, Vicki.
Perk up your ears : discover your sense of hearing / Vicki Cobb ;
illustrated by Cynthia C. Lewis.
p. cm.
ISBN 0-7613-1704-X (lib. bdg.) — ISBN 0-7613-1981-6 (pbk.)
1. Hearing. 2. Auditory perception. I. Title.
RF290 .C59 2001
612.8′5—dc21          00-068099

Text copyright © 2001 by Vicki Cobb
Illustrations copyright © 2001 by Cynthia C. Lewis
Printed in the United States of America
All rights reserved
lib:   5  4  3  2
pbk:  5  4  3  2  1

Stick your fingers in your ears. Wiggle them around. Know what you're hearing? Your fingers rubbing in your ears. Know what you're not hearing? The sounds outside the entrance to your ears.

The part of your ear that your finger is sticking into is called the *pinna*. It is like a funnel. The pinna collects sound from the air and funnels it into a canal going into your head. That's the beginning of the path sound takes to reach your brain.

Attention Students and teachers!! Harold Stout has misplaced his science project! School will be dismissed at once to allow the custodians to search for... uh.... uh... Fangs... Please line up in an orderly ...

eeEEk

Hey! This IS cool! I can't hear ANYTHING except for my fingers rubbing in my ears! Rub... rub.... rub....

Hearing is a very important sense. It warns you of dangers. It lets you enjoy music. It helps you find your way. But most importantly, it lets you understand speech. Deaf people have to learn to communicate using their sense of sight.

What happens to sound after it enters your ear? How does the brain make sense out of what you hear? Are there sounds you cannot hear? How does hearing help tell you where you are? Can you fool your sense of hearing? These are some of the questions scientists ask. They find the answers by doing experiments. When you do the experiments in this book, you are a scientist. You can investigate your own sense of hearing and that of your friends. You will all want to perk up your ears.

## THE STRUCTURE OF THE HUMAN EAR

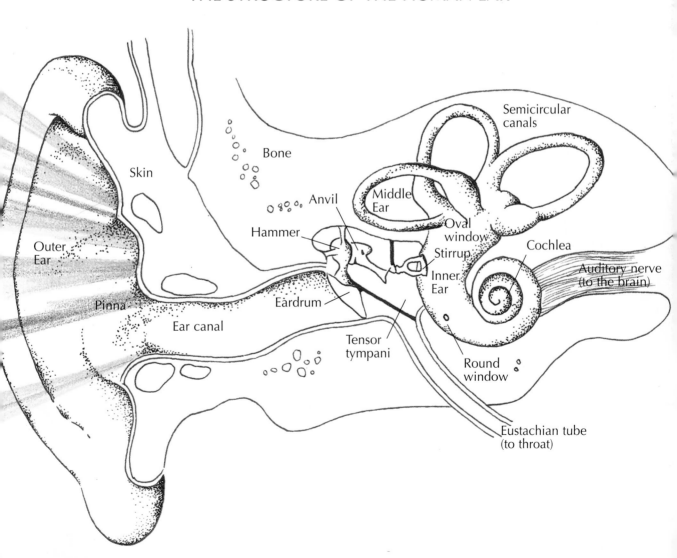

# CONDUCTING SOUND

Still got your fingers in your ears? If not, put them back in and say, "Hear this." Now take your fingers out of your ears and say it again. Notice that when your ears are plugged your voice sounds lower and fuller than it does when your ears are unplugged. That's because when your ears are plugged the sound of your voice is being conducted to your ears through your skin, muscles and bones, and not through the air.

Sound is energy that travels through matter such as air, water, wood, metal, or bone. It must have matter to travel. In a vacuum, where there is no air, there are no sounds. You have to talk on a radio on the moon, even to a person who is right next to you. Ever notice how different your voice sounds to you on a tape recorder? If you never have, make a recording on an answering machine and play it back. You are used to hearing the sound of your voice conducted through both the air and your head. Other people hear your voice only through the air. When they hear your voice on a tape recorder or an answering machine, it doesn't sound different from the way they hear you speak through the air.

Here's an experiment that shows how sound is conducted. You will need two metal forks and about 2 feet (60 centimeters) of waxed dental floss. Tie one end of the dental floss around one of the forks. Hold the other end of the floss about 12 inches (30 centimeters) above the fork, and let the fork dangle. Strike the dangling fork with the other fork.

If you listen to the sound through the air you will hear a tinny ringing. Now hold the floss between your thumb and middle finger and drape the extra floss over the tip of your index finger. Stick that finger, with the floss, into your ear, and strike the fork again. Now you hear what sounds like the deep bonging of a grandfather clock.

When you strike the fork, it starts vibrating. Vibrations are tiny, rapid, back-and-forth motions. The fork vibrations set the air and the string vibrating. The string vibrations make the bones of your head and the air in your ear canal vibrate. Everything that transmits vibrations conducts the sound to your ear. But the bones in your head conduct deeper tones than the air does.

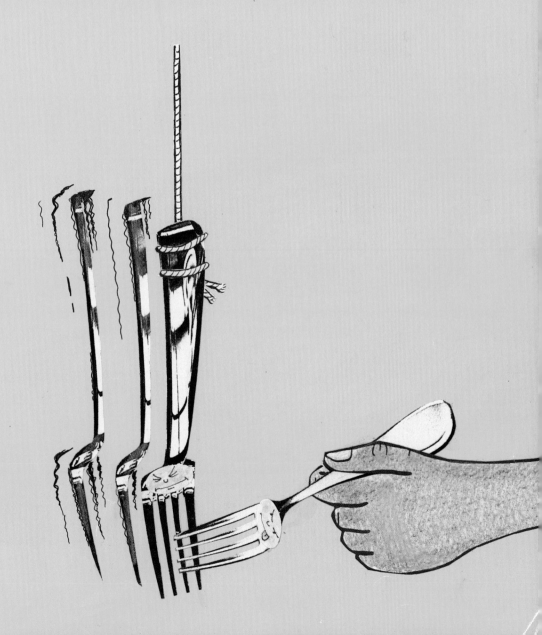

# THE AMAZING EAR

The outer ear is made up of the pinna and the ear canal. The end of the canal is closed off by a very thin "skin" called the eardrum. Sound strikes the eardrum and makes it vibrate. You can see how this happens if you stretch some plastic wrap tightly across the top of a bowl. Imagine that the stretched plastic wrap is your eardrum. Sprinkle some grains of sugar on the stretched plastic wrap drum. Clap your hands above the drum. The sugar will dance up and down as the drum vibrates. Experiment with different sounds to see how the drum responds.

"Let's see if I can get the little fellas to do the Macarena!"

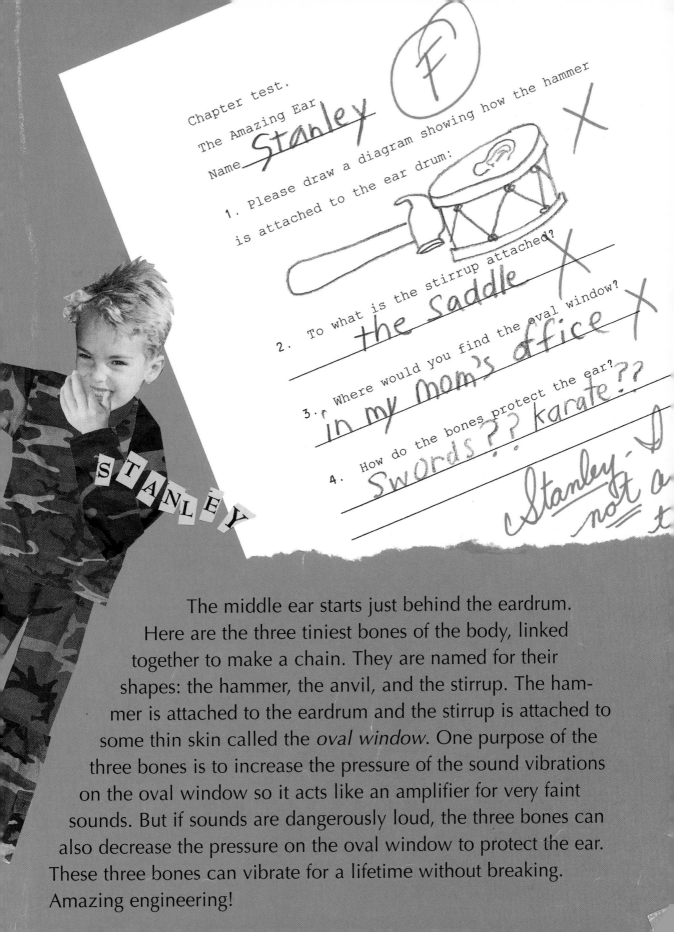

Chapter test.
The Amazing Ear

Name **Stanley**    (F)

1. Please draw a diagram showing how the hammer is attached to the ear drum:

X

2. To what is the stirrup attached?
**the saddle** X

3. Where would you find the oval window?
**in my mom's office** X

4. How do the bones protect the ear??
**swords ?? karate??**

*Stanley — I not a t*

STANLEY

The middle ear starts just behind the eardrum. Here are the three tiniest bones of the body, linked together to make a chain. They are named for their shapes: the hammer, the anvil, and the stirrup. The hammer is attached to the eardrum and the stirrup is attached to some thin skin called the *oval window*. One purpose of the three bones is to increase the pressure of the sound vibrations on the oval window so it acts like an amplifier for very faint sounds. But if sounds are dangerously loud, the three bones can also decrease the pressure on the oval window to protect the ear. These three bones can vibrate for a lifetime without breaking. Amazing engineering!

The tiny bones of the middle ear are surrounded by air. Normally, the air pressure in the middle ear is the same as the outside air pressure. When you go up in an airplane or a high-speed elevator, the air pressure on the outside of the eardrum drops. Now the air pressure in your middle ear is greater than the outside pressure on your eardrum and your ears feel clogged. Fortunately, the middle ear is connected by a tube to the back of your throat. So if you yawn, you can release the pressure in your middle ear and make it the same as your outer ear again.

The inner ear starts on the other side of the oval window. Its structure is like a snail's shell. In fact, it is called the *cochlea*, which means "shell-shaped."  It is made of three long tubes that are coiled into a spiral. The cochlea is filled with fluid. When the stirrup vibrates against the oval window, vibrations travel through the fluid, which also conducts sound. Inside the cochlea, along the walls between the tubes, are about 15,000 tiny hair cells that pick up the vibrations like tiny antennae.

Hey! That's Eric! The guy she likes!

No way! It's his brother Dan, the one with the weird laugh...

You're BoTH wrong! It's Alex from Chorus Club...

Who IS this?

Guess!

I, uh... I CAN'T!

oh, come on... you MUST know who it is...

...confused cochlea hair cells present a problem for Jennifer when she gets a phone call....

At the base of each group of hair cells are many nerve fibers that change the vibrations of the hair cells into impulses that go to the brain. When the messages reach the brain, you interpret what you are hearing.  The hair cells in the cochlea are so sensitive that you hear a tremendous variety of sounds: deep sounds, high sounds, loud and soft sounds, single notes, chords, and very complicated sounds that let you tell one person's voice from another.

Here's how you can see one way that the cochlea tells the difference between low sounds and high sounds. Imagine that your index finger is like a cochlea. Place the end of your index finger against the Adam's apple of your dad or some other friendly man. Ask him to make a loud low sound like a foghorn. Feel the vibrations go down your finger. Now ask him to make a loud high sound like a whistling teakettle. Notice that only the tip of your finger feels the vibrations. In the cochlea, the hair cells deeper into the cochlea detect lower sounds than the hair cells close to the oval window.

# TEST YOUR HEARING

How keen are your ears? Here's a way to find out. You will need a watch that ticks. Place the watch in a quiet room. Move away from the watch until you can just barely hear the sound. This is your threshold distance. Check out the threshold distances of your friends and family.

You can change your threshold distance. Go into another room and listen to some fairly loud music or a TV for about ten minutes. Then go check your threshold distance again. Do you have to stand closer or farther away from the watch to hear it? How does the hearing of older people compare to kids' hearing?

Sounds are measured in *decibels,* dB for short. Perfect silence is 0 dB. A whisper is 15 dB and normal conversation is about 60 dB or about 10,000 times louder than the whisper. A lawn mower, at 90 dB, is 1,000 times louder than conversation. A rock concert or a jet engine at 120 dB is 1,000,000 times louder than conversation. Anything above 85 dB can damage your ears, especially if the sound continues over a period of time.

Airport workers wear ear protection. But people attending rock concerts don't. If you've ever listened to very loud music, you may notice a ringing in your ears and soreness the next day. If you make a habit of listening to such loud sounds, you may suffer permanent hearing loss.

why attending rock concerts can be dangerous...

Hey Jake, how was the rock concert last night? ....HELLO?! ...Oh, I guess you can't hear very well today.... So, uh... I think I'll take some of your CDs over to Katie's house... and I figure I'll get there on your new bike and borrow $20 or so from you in case Katie wants to sell me her 4 gerbils and w'...

As you lose your hearing, your ability to hear very high tones is the first to go. Here's how you can test this. Turn on a television set and turn the volume all the way down or put it on mute. Lean over the back of the set and listen for a soft, high-pitched whine. If you can hear it, you are listening to sound that is in the highest range of human hearing. Walk away from it to determine your distance threshold.

Wayne's parents never really understood their budding young scientist...

Wayne! The little man isn't REALLY inside the television, dear!

Test other members of your family and friends. Test people of different ages. In general, most older people will have lost the ability to hear these high sounds. How well do teenage rock-music fans do?

# TWO EARS ARE BETTER THAN ONE

How good are you at telling where a sound is coming from? Close your eyes and have a friend clap hands at different places around you. Each time, see if you can point to the source of the sound. You're pretty good at it, aren't you? Now stick your finger in one ear, close your eyes and try again. It's a lot harder to locate the sound, isn't it?

Here's why. Most of the time a sound is closer to one ear than the other. So sound reaches one ear a split second before it reaches the other. Your sense of hearing can detect this tiny difference, which your brain interprets as the location of the sound. What happens when the sound is the same distance from both ears? With your eyes closed have someone clap directly behind you and then directly over your head. Not so easy this time, is it?

♪♫F♩♩
"Happy Birthday
to you…"

What happens to your ability to locate sounds under water? Next time you take a bath, experiment and find out. Close your eyes and have someone tap the side of the tub while your head is above water. You should have no trouble locating the sound. Now close your eyes, hold your breath, and go underwater. Have the tub tapped somewhere also underwater. The location of the sound should be much harder to place. That's because sound travels much faster in water than in air, and the difference between the times the sound reaches each ear is too close for your ears to detect the direction.

Some of the sounds made by whales are so low that humans can't hear them. Their songs travel long distances under water.

Even after Henry left his parents and got his own pod, he heard from them quite often.

Bats make sounds that bounce off the things around them. By listening for these bounced sounds, or echoes, they can find their way. This type of navigation is called *echolocation.* You can do it, too. You need a friend to help. Here's how to do it. Put on a blindfold so that you can't even see light or dark. (You might want to turn out the lights.) Have your friend take you to the middle of an uncluttered room or hallway and face you toward a wall. Start saying the word "hello" over and over again as you walk slowly toward the wall. Try to stop right before you make contact with the wall. (Your friend should watch to make sure you don't get hurt.)

Try it again from a different location in the room, but facing the same wall. You don't want to be able to count steps. Scientists have discovered that most people get good at echolocation with about five minutes of practice. Many blind people have become so good at echolocation that they can detect the size and shape of objects and rooms. Once you feel comfortable doing this, try it again, only this time cover your ears and don't speak. Can you see the difference echolocation makes in finding your way?

# NAME THAT SOUND

A key turning in a lock, the beep of a microwave, a drop of water hitting a sink are a few of the thousands of different sounds that have special meaning for you. Your ears can be trained to identify differences in sounds that may be very much alike. Take the familiar sound of a hand clap. There are four different ways you can clap your hands:

1. Palms flat and facing each other
2. Palms flat and crossed
3. Palms cupped and crossed
4. Fingers only on the palm of the other hand

Close your eyes and listen to a friend clap hands with different hand positions. See if you can name which way the hands are clapped.

Your sense of hearing can be trained to sort pennies. Get a bunch of pennies and sort them into two piles by looking at the dates. One pile should include pennies from 1982 and older; the other should include 1983 and newer.

Now for the training session. Ask a friend to pick a penny from one group and tell you which group the penny came from. The penny should be dropped on a hard, tile floor while you close your eyes and listen. After a while you will be able to

tell the difference. The newer pennies will have a dull, tinny sound. The older pennies make a sharper, ringing sound. This is because in 1983 the U.S. government decided to cut costs by adding some zinc to the melted copper that was minted into pennies. The zinc-copper pennies look the same as the pure copper ones, but your "cents" of hearing can learn to detect the difference when they're dropped.

# DON'T BELIEVE YOUR EARS

What happens when you say the word "say" aloud over and over again? Keep it up long enough and it no longer is the word "say." It becomes the word "ace." Keep saying "ace" aloud over and over again and it becomes the word "say" again. You have no control over when the word changes.

This is called an "alternating form" illusion. The first sound of the word "say" becomes the last sound of the new word "ace." When you repeat the words aloud, they run together. You are not giving your brain enough clues as to which is the first sound and which is the last. So your brain reorganizes the sound without you trying. After a while it reorganizes again and you hear the original word. This will continue as long as you keep saying the words. Another word you might try is "stress." What word does it become?

When you listen to someone talk, how important is it to see the lips move? Do an experiment to find out. Find a news program or a talk show on TV. Turn down the volume as you watch the speaker's face. Keep lowering the volume until you can just barely hear the speaker. Close your eyes. Can you understand what's being said? Open your eyes and watch the speaker. Is it easier to get the message now?

We all watch people's lips to help us understand what they are saying. This is especially true when it is hard to hear the person. Sight is the dominant sense in human beings. We believe our eyes before we believe our ears. Do the next lip reading experiment to see how.

You will need two friends to do this. One of them should not know what's going to happen. This person will be the subject of your experiment. The subject should face you and your other friend should crouch behind you. On the count of three you silently mouth the word "vase" over and over again exaggerating the "V." At the same time, the friend behind you should say the word "base" aloud over and over again. It is very important that the word "base" should be synchronized with your lips mouthing the word "vase." After about eight repetitions ask the subject what he or she hears. Most likely it is the word "vase." Now ask you what word is heard when the eyes are closed. Your subject should have no problem hearing the spoken word "base."

Try it again with you mouthing the word "gate" while your friend speaks the word "bait." It's possible that your subject hears the word "date." Try it and see.

# GIFTED EARS

Who are the most finely tuned listeners? Musicians, probably, especially the ones with perfect pitch. Musical notes are named with letters of the alphabet: A, B, C, D, E, F, and G. Half-tones between notes are called sharps and flats. People who can hear any musical note and identify it by name are said to have perfect pitch. They can also sing any note you ask them to produce without hearing any other notes. Many composers, including Mozart and Beethoven, have had perfect pitch. When Mozart was seven years old, he said that his violin was tuned slightly higher than another violin belonging to his father's friend. When they checked violins, they found that little Mozart was right. Some people with perfect pitch can tell what pitch a bird sings, what pitch the wind makes, and the pitch of a nose being blown. Perfect pitch is very rare. Less than one person in every 10,000 has it.

You can be tested to see if you or your friends have perfect pitch. Of course, you must know the notes of the scale in order to do this. The person doing the testing sits at a piano and plays a note. The person being tested tries to name the note.

If you can carry a tune, you have the beginning of relative pitch. Relative pitch means that once you know one note, you can find another. The more you involve yourself with music by playing an instrument or singing, the better your hearing gets and the more pleasure you get from your ears. Perk up your ears and enjoy the world of sounds around you.

## ABOUT THE AUTHOR

Vicki Cobb loves her sense of hearing, because with it she can hear people clapping when she finishes giving a presentation in schools. She can also hear people say nice things about her books. She would like to hear somebody say "You've just won a million dollars," but she hasn't heard that yet. You can visit Vicki at www.vickicobb.com.

## ABOUT THE ILLUSTRATOR

Cynthia Lewis probably uses her sense of hearing more when she's working on her artwork than she does at other times. This is because she works all the way upstairs and needs to listen to what's going on with her children who are all the way downstairs. Luckily, Cindy has a very good sense of hearing, and very good, sensible kids.